SHATTERED STORIES

WASHIMA NARZISH

This book is dedicated to each and every person of my life who appreciates me for writing and always stands by me in ups and downs of life.

Contents

Contents

Preface

This is my first book. Poems and tales about of this book are imaginary, related to new topics which everyone can relate to. Somehow, certain poems are based on experience, longing for purity of love and the feeling of missing one's own home and certain poems are about friendship, reunion and the last day of college diary.

Acknowledgements

First of all, I would like to thank my readers. Without them, a writer or a poet is totally incomplete and of course, I would like to thank my family and teachers for their guidance and my friends for their support. This book is a hope, a dream for me.

Thank you, dear Kaveri Ba for the edits and helping me to publish this book, you converted one of my biggest dreams into reality.

This book is a test of my patience too.

Prologue

This book is about love, friendship, reunion, lost moments, memories, unexplainable emotions, second chances given by life, etc. So, my dear lovely readers please go through the book and never forget to give me your valuable feedbacks. Each poem has it's own uniqueness and versatility .

1. Reunion

After so long, we reunited...
From changed time to changed faces.
Unexplainable happiness that we preserved
in the last pages of our college books.
Maybe, that day somehow the
bitter-sweet friendship of us
revived once again.
Our lost stories, lost friendship,
lost love and half-written poems
again reunited, through a handshake
and a short span of hug.
Was it a formality?
Tell me if someone cares.
It was our 'reunion' after all.

2. Is that girl fragile?

She is sensitive. She is bold.
Yet, she is numb sometimes.
You should also know, she has her own identity
and she fights for equality.
Her own melody is like that extraordinary cassette.
Her soulful music tends to flow in an undefined way.
She is a girl with utmost desire,
a believer within a never ending loop.
She is a girl with versatility, who will grow
and glow in her own way immensely.

3. Hallucinogenic Love

Two broken souls in the burning phase of love,
longing and desiring for the trauma throughout.
Their messy hairs, their hazardous tears
after a few unpleasant years.
Nothing else butjust a bulk of freezing
emotions in a worthless summer night.

4. A bit of nostalgia

Somewhere nostalgia strikes tonight.
Nostalgia from the past.
It was from a decade or an era ago.
It was that time when everything was different.
He said, "Let's talk to the depth of our souls
along with a cup of hot tea."
Then we talked about the moon, stars, sunset,
waterfall and rain.
We memorized each other's words like poems.
Still, something was missing that day,
something was strange and unknown.
Now, look yesterday we created a memory and
now it remains as nostalgic as the deadly frozen poetry.

5. She

She is an art,
someone's muse and creation.
She is an irreplaceable part of old melodies.
Yes, she is a masterpiece.
Yet, she is sophisticated and
contradiction of love.

6. Shattered

An egregious person you were,
when we first met.
You were at the highest altitude of life.
But my daydreams of loving you and
nightmares of losing you swiftly turned
into a reality of mine.
I guess you did not know the vulnerability
of a shattered soul.
The messed up thoughts and fake euphoria
is called shattered.
Being shattered is inconceivable and tragic.
Shattered refers to the moments of lost aroma
and the birth of mysterious poems.
And of course,
shattered stands for me and you.

7. Strangers again

From sharing a cup of tea to sharing lot of talks.
From faded destruction to a blissful ending
may not be a 'happily ever after'.
A story where we reunited so quickly.
Still, my deadly driven soul wants your existence
as a treasure, as an epitome of peace and
as an aroma of wildflower, literally free and bold.

8. Interaction

Some people get replaced at times.
New comers teach how to live the actual worth of life.
I am seeking for comfort, seeking for peace as if it feels like home.
A long hug and a bit of understanding which will
vivify our souls.
Human beings are the theme of exploring, knowing and
judging each other.
Some of them are easier to understand or resolve.
Few others are filled up with regret.
Still, life goes on no matter what.

9. Again us

Let's occupy our empty spaces with burning desires.
Let's try to understand each other, if you want!
Let's allow our vibes to coincide or reconnect.
Let's burn all the shades of hatred we ever had.
We were those petals of tulip flower which were
totally into itself.
Hopefully, it was that specific day towards a new journey.
Those beautiful stories where each and every
reviving thoughts of mine are going to define you...
For sure!!

10. Soulmate

Fragrance of lavender flowers will heal
our half written thoughts.
Petals of love between us can be better
than the day before yesterday.
This will be an era.
Era with your unexplainable love.
The era with an exquisite soulmate

11. Alternation

Can all the parts of hatred between us be unaltered?
Where are we driving towards now?
The unsaid parts of my soul longs for your sanity, even without
your presence, sometimes.
Don't know why but unsaid parts say a lot and
unsaid talks define us a lot.

12. The sea and the sky

The depth of the sea equals to the height of the sky,
for me when you hold my hands.
A soul like mine passes through the moonlight and
the delightful sunset, when you are with me.
The sea with it's million little dreams forms a
parallel world with the sky which has infinite love series.

13. Breeze of love

An empty road during a starry night,
with an expectation of an everlasting
companionship, this time.
You are that specific soul who vibes with
my happiness and sorrow everytime.
You are someone who understands the poems
on moonlight and someone who dances with me
in the rain and stares at my eyes upto infinite.

14. Scene after a separation

Let's end this happily.
We must end those trouble, trauma and
hatred for our peace.
If something isn't working, let's break it down,
without any restrictions and without any queries.
Let's deal with the place where our peace leads to...
Let's find out where vibes are going to reach at it's peak.
Without judging and bullying, let's just end the nuisance.
Let's leave the place where we never felt happy and
move on to the point of satisfaction.
Time can heal everything.
Just never ask if I am okay or not till that time comes.

15. Naked Soul

Those eyes can't say anything now but those hopeless
scars are always ready to leave someone in fear.
Messed up?
But, she needs some space.
Well...she dressed up like a hoe?
Still,
her ugliness to pitiful eyes can't give you any explanation now.
Judging someone is a popular term in today's generation.
And body shaming to bullying, is it observance?
Somewhere, this period is so judgmental.
Isn't it?

16. Muse

I saw you in an artistic way at first sight.
So, preserved you like an unforgettable
aroma of love yet.
Yes...
I painted you like the specific sketches
of forts and religious beliefs, where, I captured
you like the monuments of aesthetic places.
Ofcourse,
I recited you like my story,
which vivifies my soul after the ages.

17. Men

You always play better roles to heal or sometimes deal.
You support the whole society.
Your intelligence, your loyalties, your happiness
measure someone's soul of love.
Gentlemen,
you deserve a lot of respect.
A safe place you are for the society or for us.
Kind of support system, you are!!

18. A worthy evening

Those cherry blossoms, mountains, rivers and
a long journey with the sunset.
A deep discussion with your write-ups and
mysterious diary.
Maybe, that's where I started to write my first poem.
Time, tales and lots of talks.
What a worthy evening it was!

19. Photograph

Prolonged moments and memories measured
through these uncaptured photographs.
Perhaps happiness is enclosed between these
sweet and bitter photographs.
The period of college to hostel days are collaborating
through these bubbly photographs.
Changing age to changing era are sustaining
through these serene photographs.
Somehow,
why...I mean why,
these photographs feel more than diamonds or treasure?

20. Beloved

An empty vessel without wine,
ashes without cigarettes,
books without sentences and
a life without intense emotions
and a little bit of glorification.
Your rhythmic verse without lyrics,
I have seen it all.
Ohh man!
We have come so far.
Eye contacts, those numb eyelashes,
droplets of tears during a heavy rainfall.
The songs recommended by you
are still on my playlist...
Still!
Those songs were as favorite as you.
From detachment to attachment,
from love to tranquility of hatred
and from sharing our playlist
to sharing nothing at all.
Right now, everything is a pathetic phase,
just like you...

21. Home

Home is a place where your soul reflects,
the total amount of happiness via your face and smile.
It is that place where actual versatility
of peace describes new thoughts and moments.
Home is a place where you can find your juvenile phase
to childhood throughout lots of memories and the
last page of your notebook.
Home is a place of relief where all the sweet moments
to memories are to be cherished.
Home and hope are same where happiness is celebrated
without any occasion.

22. Saudade

Let's meet somewhere.
Let's occupy those empty phases of life,
which was not paraphrased and still reflects.
Let's cooperate our souls like those 80's retro movies.
Saudade, for sure, without any destination.

23. Us

Us…
Soothing music, sensible movies
and our vibes.
Us…
The midnight and
the worth of existence.
Us…
The rare, aesthetic poetic urge,
serenity, solace and the regrets of life.
Still, I just love seeing you through
the moonlight and dark night's paradise.
Us…
Undoubtedly mad us and hopelessly curious us.
Us…
Hallucinogenic tired eyes and your
favorite book's last page.
That was the 'us' moment, silly but
quite irreplaceable.

24. Somewhere

We are apart, just like the fountains and the sunsets.
Still double cross each other's minds like the
deepest consequences of solo music albums,
where unsaid parts requisite itself.
We are the mysterious tales, hidden thoughts
and a bit of tranquil.
Aren't these enough to getting deeper into
each other's bombarded souls?

25. First eve of Christmas

Snowy paths, cold spiffy air
and a piece of mysterious
interaction with fire.
Thorns of roses and tales
of daffodils coincide itself
unacceptably and initially.
Half of the sadness was
falling aside that day.
Still,
her dazzling eyes expressed more.
But that was the time of
closing the 'Church Gate'.
Nothing more,
just two strangers were expecting
something from each other.

26. Dissolution

The smell of your cigarettes
with your smoky, teary eyes,
that I missed a lot.
The tranquility of your lips
in which I was addicted.
I think my life needs that thing
more and more, now and forever.
The troublesome, terrific tides
throughout Nirvana's music.
Undoubtedly we were lost
in different directions !!

27. A silly thought

*Memories of unvisualized things affect
everyone else unknowingly.
Do you know, at that phase neither
you were perfect nor was I?
Watching moon light to sunset altogether.
Maybe we grew up in an unpredictable era.
Maybe for a while, we were together.
But, neither you were accompanied by me
nor was I accompanied by you.*

28. Will you be my October?

Will you be my October?
The season of grace with siuli.
Will you be my season of innumerable
moments of happiness?
Will you be those tales
of imaginary world and the
sparkle inside happiness?
The season of glorious vibe
for a little while.
I wish I could dance on
this season of October.
I wish I could able to recolor
the fragrance of happiness
twice or more than that.
Autumn is coming
and this year autumn is
going to stay for litte longer.
But, should we stay as well?

29. Live a little more

Something is unpredictable here,
in this world of unbounded loop,
in this puzzling phase of the
phenomenological place.
Moments should be cherished and
unknown places should be explored.
Sometimes, live a little more
for yourself, by yourself.

30. Sunset and ice

From these unread novels to
those old photographs.
From those hilly areas to breeze of
love with a lot of memories.
From poetry writing to
unsaid paragraphs of our story,
which is left as a hurtful sorrow now.
It is the actual combination
of sunset and ice,
opposite but unidirectional.

31. Perfection

She was as perfect as I thought,
the way she talked,
the way she walked,
the way she disappeared
and the way she put her mascara
on her eyelashes.
She was as wild as I thought.
Her dank, crazy and
surprising eyes expressed a lot.
We were at the
point of hell and the
highest altitude of regression.
She was literally as artistic as I thought.

32. Desirable Fantasy

Ancient vista of songs and us
vibing with our deepest souls.
Forgetting that unpleasant place
and past that once existed.
How adorable would our pathways
have been if we met earlier...
We were so helpless at that time.
Look at us now,
uplifting each other politely
upto infinity.

33. Old cassette

Into the woods,
into the serenity,
somewhere lost between the
moments and magnificent life.
The lost aroma of a
questionnaire sequence.
That old cassette is still my favorite,
which was gifted by you.

34. Friday Night

Last year on this day,
we shared half of each part of that diary.
Maybe it is called a bit of 'love'.
My half written paragraphs and
laterally overlapped thoughts
somewhere hit that day hardest the most.
Do you still remember?
Yeah! It is friday night today.
Too late to receive a
last goodbye from you.

35. Beauty of life

*This urge to fall in love with
your vibes, underrated places,
rivers with the soulful songs and
tunes of guitar again and again.
Staring at the dark night,
watching underrated movies
with someone special.
Falling in love with yourself again
like you are now sixteen.
Falling in love with your own writings
and his poems like it's contemporary.
Falling in love with raindrops or lightning,
no matter how much terrible it is.
Falling in love with the meaningful lyrics and
the characters which don't even exist.
This urge to fall in love with the downstairs of
Temple, Church and Masjid once again...*

36. A wish

I wish I could admit it
after the demise of someone close,
"Return if possible rather than
resting in peace."
Radiate positivity with your good deeds,
even if the world must have been
a cruel place to live in.
Just a wish to say,
"Return if possible rather
than resting in peace".

37. Electro-Versatility

Peace can be amplified,
world can be rectified,
my mind is still driving through
the actual way of your transducer.
Don't know the reason why...
Only you can control that crazy
sinusoidal vibes of mine, within
certain amount of potential difference.
My resistivity to retentivity,
towards hope and expectation
is falling aside.
Still...
Wavelets of highly oriented amplifier
wants only you, in my beside.
PS : Author is pursuing Electrical Engineering.

38. A hazy eve

An empty evening without someone.
An empty thought without paper and ink.
It's just tiny tales with the moonlight
and twilight of an aesthetic scenario.
When death becomes a poetry,
you are indeed obsessed with it.
Obsessed with it more,
rather than shattered and terrific life

39. The last days of sparkle

*From the season of introducing ourselves
to one another to the days of interacting for
such long periods of time...
Days went so fast.
The days of gazing into each other's eyes
turned into sweet little memories at present.
But,
it is the blossom of farewell now.
The softness of bitter-sweet moments,
tears of sadness and joy,
collaboration with new lives and
the beginning of a new journey ahead.
Capturing moments to rejoicing those
pieces of memories today.
This box of treasure will never fade away.
Time flows...
Glittery events of farewell happens.
Then, the hardest goodbye and solace
of reinventing the self takes place.*

40. Indication

Once again, let me fall in
love with a stranger.
What would you say?
Like a lost wanderer,
let's allows our souls
to vibe with new songs,
new movies and new places.
This is the new journey.
The journey of ourselves,
after a breakdown,
after a crossover...